PSYCHOLOGY OF ATTACHMENT

Timeless guides, facts and secrets on the science of Child and Adult Attachment, how to determine your Attachment pattern/style and how they affect Adult Codependency and Relationships

George Graham.

Copyright©2022George Graham

All Rights Reserved.

TABLE OF CONTENTS

TABLE OF CONTENTS	2
INTRODUCTION	5
CHAPTER ONE	11
Attachment Theory	11
CHAPTER TWO	21
Attachment Behaviors	21
CHAPTER THREE	27
The Independency Bluff	27
CHAPTER FOUR	35
Attachment Patterns/Styles	35
Secure Attachment	36
Anxious Attachment	37
Avoidant Attachment	39
Fearful-Avoidant Attachment (Disorganized)	41
CHAPTER FIVE	43
Attachment Pattern/Styles in Adults	43
Securely Attached	43
Anxious-Preoccupied	44
Dismissive-Avoidant	45

    Fearful-Avoidant   47

CHAPTER SIX   49

  How to Identify your Attachment Style/Pattern   49

    Secure Attachment Style   50

    Avoidant Attachment Style   51

    Anxious Attachment Style   53

    Disorganized Attachment Style   55

CHAPTER SEVEN   57

  How your Attachment Pattern/Style affects your Relationship   57

    How Secure Attachment Style appears in Relationships   58

    How Avoidant Attachment Style appears in Relationships   59

    How Anxious Attachment Style appears in Relationships   60

    How Disorganized Attachment Style manifests in Relationships   61

CHAPTER EIGHT   63

  Assessing and Measuring Attachment   63

    Associations of Adult Attachment with other Traits   64

CHAPTER NINE   65

    Can your Attachment Style change?   65

       Distinguish your relationship patterns.   65

       Work on your Confidence.   66

       Reach out to your genuine requirements.   67

       Feel free to seek therapy.   67

CONCLUSION   69

INTRODUCTION

Attachment implies a fondness bond or tie between an individual and an attachment figure (normally a guardian). Such bonds might be equal between two grown-ups, yet between a youngster and a parental figure, these bonds depend on the kid's requirement for wellbeing, security, and security — which is most significant in earliest stages and youth.

Attachment Theory is definitely not a thorough portrayal of human relationships, nor is it inseparable from adoration and fondness, albeit these may demonstrate that securities exist. In kid to-grown-up Attachments, the kid's tie is known as the "Attachment" and the guardian's corresponding comparable is alluded to as the "care-giving bond".

Attachment styles allude to the specific manner by which an individual connects with others. The idea includes one's trust in the accessibility of the attachment figure for use as a solid base from which one can uninhibitedly investigate the world when not in trouble as well as a place of refuge from which one can look for help, security, and solace in the midst of pain.

In humans, the Attachment social framework doesn't close in early stages, or even adolescence, yet rather is dynamic all through the life expectancy, with people acquiring solace from both physical and mental portrayals of soul mates.

There seems, by all accounts, to be progression between early attachment styles and the nature of later grown-up close attachments. This thought depends on the inward working model where a baby's essential attachment frames a model (layout) for future attachments.

Attachment Theory depends on the statement that there should be in a cozy relationship is implanted in our qualities. We've been modified by development to single out a couple of explicit people in our lives and make them valuable to us. We've been reproduced to be reliant upon a critical other. The need begins in the belly and finishes when we bite the dust. All through development, hereditary determination inclined toward individuals who became joined on the grounds that it gave an endurance advantage.

In ancient times, individuals who depended exclusively on themselves and had nobody to safeguard them were bound to wind up as prey. Generally, the people who were with someone who profoundly thought often about them made due to give to their posterity the inclination to frame cozy bonds. As a matter of fact, the should be close to somebody unique is vital to the point that the cerebrum has an organic system explicitly liable for making and directing our association with our Attachment figures (guardians, kids, and significant others). This instrument, called the Attachment framework, comprises of feelings and ways of behaving that guarantee that we stay protected and safeguarded by remaining nearby our friends and family. The system makes sense of why a kid separated from their mom ends up being rushed, look fiercely, or cries wildly until the person restores contact with her.

These responses are instituted protest behavior; we as a whole actually display them as adults. In ancient times, being near an partner involved life and demise, and our attachment framework created to regard such closeness as an outright need.

A critical part of advancement is heterogeneity. Humans are exceptionally heterogeneous animal types, differing enormously for all intents and purposes, mentalities, and ways of behaving. This records generally for our overflow and for our capacity to squeeze into practically any biological specialty on the planet. In the event that we were all indistinguishable, any single natural test would and can possibly wipe us full scale. Our fluctuation further develops the possibilities that a portion of the populace that is novel somehow or another could endure when others wouldn't. Attachment style is the same as some other human trademark. Despite the fact that we as a whole have an essential need to shape close bonds, the manner in which we make them shifts. In an exceptionally perilous climate, it would be less profitable to put investment in only one individual since the person in question wouldn't probably be around for a really long time; it would check out to get less connected and continue on (and subsequently, the avoidant Attachment style).

One more choice in an unforgiving climate is to act in the contrary way and be seriously determined and hyper-cautious about remaining nearby your attachment figure (consequently, the Anxious Attachment style). In a more quiet setting, the personal securities framed by putting enormously in a specific individual would yield more noteworthy advantages for both the individual and their posterity (consequently, the solid Attachment style).

Valid, in current culture, we are not pursued by hunters as our progenitors were; however in developmental terms we're just a negligible portion of a second from the old plan of things. Our profound cerebrum was given over to us by Homo sapiens who lived in something else entirely, and it is their way of life and the risks they experienced that our feelings were intended to address. Our sentiments and ways of behaving in attachments today are not very different from those of our initial precursors.

CHAPTER ONE

Attachment Theory

Attachment Theory is a mental, developmental and ethological theory concerning attachments between people. The main principle is that small kids need to foster a relationship with something like one essential guardian for typical social and close to home turn of events. The Theory was figured out by specialist and psychoanalyst John Bowlby.

Inside Attachment Theory, baby conduct related with attachment is principally the looking for of closeness to an attachment figure in unpleasant circumstances. Babies become connected to grown-ups who are delicate and responsive in friendly co-operations with them, and who stay as predictable guardians for certain months during the period from around a half year to two years old. During the last option part of this period, youngsters start to utilize Attachment figures (natural individuals) as a solid base to investigate from and return to. Parental reactions lead to the advancement of examples of Attachment; these, thusly, lead to interior working models which will direct the individual's sentiments, considerations and assumptions in later relationships. Fear of abandonment following the deficiency of a attachment figure is viewed as a typical and versatile reaction for a attached newborn child. These ways of behaving may have developed on the grounds that they increment the likelihood of survival of the kid.

Inside Attachment Theory, Attachment implies an affection bond or tie between an individual and a Attachment figure (normally a guardian). Such bonds might be proportional between two grown-ups, yet between a kid and a guardian, these bonds depend on the youngster's requirement for wellbeing, security, and security — which is most significant in earliest stages and youth. Attachment Theory is definitely not a comprehensive portrayal of human Attachments, nor is it inseparable from adoration and fondness, albeit these may demonstrate that securities exist. In kid to-grown-up Attachments, the youngster's tie is known as the "Attachment" and the parental figure's corresponding comparable is alluded to as the "care-giving bond". The Theory suggests that youngsters connect to carers naturally, with the end goal of endurance and, at last, hereditary replication. The organic point is endurance and the mental point is security. The relationship that a kid has with their attachment figure is particularly significant in undermining circumstances. Approaching a protected figure diminishes dread in kids when they are given undermining circumstances. Not exclusively is having a diminished degree of dread significant for general mental soundness, yet it likewise involves how kids could respond to undermining circumstances. The presence of a steady attachment figure is particularly significant in a kid's formative years.

Babies will shape attachments to any predictable parental figure who is delicate and responsive in friendly collaborations with them. The nature of social commitment is more powerful than how much time spent. The natural mother is the standard head attachment figure, however the job can be taken by any individual who reliably acts in a "mothering" far throughout some undefined time frame. Inside Attachment Theory, this implies a bunch of ways of behaving that includes taking part in vivacious social collaboration with the baby and answering promptly to signs and approaches. Nothing in the Theory recommends that fathers are not similarly prone to become head attachment assumes if they give a large portion of the kid care and related social collaboration. A solid attachment with to a dad "optional attachment figure" may likewise a counter the conceivable negative effects of an unacceptable attachment to the essential mother attachment figure.

A few babies direct Attachment conduct (vicinity chasing) towards more than one Attachment figure nearly when they begin to show separation between guardians; generally come to do as such during their subsequent year. These figures are organized progressively, with the vital Attachment figure at the top. The put forth objective of the Attachment conduct framework is to keep a bond with an open and accessible Attachment figure. "Alert" is the term utilized for enactment of the Attachment social framework brought about by dread of risk. "Uneasiness" is the expectation or anxiety toward being cut off from the Attachment figure. On the off chance that the figure is inaccessible or lethargic, detachment trouble happens. In babies, actual division can cause uneasiness and outrage, trailed by trouble and despondency. By age three or four, actual partition is at this point not such a danger to the kid's bond with the Attachment figure. Dangers to security in more established kids and grown-ups emerge from delayed nonattendance, breakdowns in correspondence, close to home inaccessibility or indications of dismissal or deserting.

Attachment Theory assigns three fundamental "Attachment styles," or habits in which individuals see and answer closeness in heartfelt Attachments, which equal those tracked down in youngsters: Secure, Anxious, and Avoidant. Fundamentally, secure individuals feel OK with closeness and are generally warm and cherishing; Anxious individuals desire closeness, are frequently distracted with their Attachments, and will quite often stress over their partner's capacity to cherish them back; avoidant individuals liken closeness with a deficiency of freedom and continually attempt to limit closeness.

In addition, people with each of these attachment styles differ in:

- Their view of intimacy and togetherness
- The manner in which they manage struggle
- Their mentality toward sex

- Their capacity to convey their desires and needs.
- Their assumptions from their partner and the relationship

All individuals in our general public, whether they have quite recently begun dating somebody or have been hitched for a very long time, can be categorized as one of these classifications, or, all the more once in a blue moon, into a mix of the last two (anxious and avoidant). A little more than 50% are secure, around 20% are anxious, 25% are avoidant, and the excess 3 to 5 percent fall into a fourth, more uncommon complicated class.

Throughout recent many years, grown-up attachment research has created many logical papers and many books that cautiously outline the manner by which grown-ups act in close heartfelt ties. These examinations have affirmed, many times over, the presence of these attachment styles in grown-ups in a large number of nations and societies, including the US, Australia, Canada, Germany, Israel, Italy, Portugal, the Netherlands, and the Unified Realm.

Understanding Attachment styles is a simple and solid method for understanding and foreseeing individuals' conduct in any heartfelt circumstance.

As a matter of fact, one of the primary messages of this theory is that in heartfelt circumstances, we are customized to act in a foreordained way.

Attachment Theory was formed based on the populace at large. Attachment Theory drew its examples from everybody — the people who have blissful attachments and the individuals who don't, the people who never seek treatment and the people who effectively look for it. It permitted us to learn what goes "wrong" in Attachments yet additionally what goes "right," and it permitted us to find and feature an entire gathering who are scarcely referenced in most relationship books. Additionally, the Theory doesn't name ways of behaving as solid or undesirable. None of the Attachment styles is in itself seen as "pathological." Running against the norm, heartfelt ways of behaving that had recently been viewed as odd or misinformed now appeared to be justifiable, unsurprising, even anticipated. You stay with somebody in spite of the fact that he doesn't know he adores you? Justifiable. You say you need to leave and a couple of moments later adjust your perspective and conclude that you frantically need to remain? Reasonable as well.

However, are such ways of behaving successful or advantageous? That is an alternate story. Individuals with a protected Attachment style know how to convey their own assumptions and answer their partner's necessities successfully without falling back on fight conduct. Until the end of us, understanding is just the start.

Attachment Theory is an overall Theory of heartfelt association that considers the improvement of helpful applications for individuals in all phases of their heartfelt life. There are explicit applications for individuals who are dating, those in beginning phases of Attachments, and the people who are in long haul ones, for individuals going through a separation or the individuals who are lamenting the departure of a friend or family member.

The ongoing idea is that Attachment Theory can be put to strong use in these circumstances and can assist with directing individuals all through their lives to better Attachments.

Outfitted with our new bits of knowledge about the ramifications of Attachment styles in daily existence, we began to see individuals' activities in an unexpected way. Ways of behaving that were credited to somebody's character qualities, or that we had recently named as misrepresented, could now be perceived with lucidity and accuracy from the perspective of Attachment Theory.

By understanding that individuals shift significantly in their requirement for closeness and closeness, and that these distinctions make conflicts, Attachment discoveries offered us a better approach for checking heartfelt Attachments out.

CHAPTER TWO

Attachment Behaviors

Insecure Attachment examples can think twice about and the accomplishment of fearlessness. A securely connected child is allowed to focus on their current circumstance.

The Attachment conduct framework serves to accomplish or keep up with closeness to the Attachment figure. Pre-Attachment ways of behaving happen in the initial a half year of life. During the main stage (the initial two months), newborn children grin, prattle, and cry to draw in the consideration of possible parental figures. Despite the fact that babies of this age figure out how to separate between guardians, these ways of behaving are aimed at anybody nearby.

During the subsequent stage (two to a half year), the baby separates among natural and new grown-ups, turning out to be more responsive toward the guardian; following and gripping are added to the scope of ways of behaving. The baby's way of behaving toward the guardian becomes coordinated on an objective guided premise to accomplish the circumstances that encourage it

Toward the finish of the principal year, the baby can show a scope of Attachment ways of behaving intended to keep up with vicinity. These manifest as fighting the guardian's takeoff, welcoming the parental figure's return, gripping when scared, and following when capable.

With the improvement of motion, the baby starts to utilize the guardian or parental figures as a "protected base" from which to investigate. Newborn child investigation is more noteworthy when the guardian is available in light of the fact that the baby's Attachment framework is loose and it is allowed to investigate. In the event that the guardian is difficult to reach or lethargic, Attachment conduct is all the more firmly shown. Uneasiness, dread, sickness, and weakness will make a kid increment Attachment ways of behaving.

After the subsequent year, as the kid sees the guardian as a free individual, a more perplexing and objective revised organization is shaped.

Youngsters start to appropriately see others' objectives and sentiments and plan their activities.

Present day Attachment Theory depends on three standards:

- Holding is a natural human need.
- Guideline of feeling and dread to improve essentialness.
- Advancing a versatile nature and development.

Normal Attachment ways of behaving and feelings, showed in most friendly primates including people, are versatile. The drawn out advancement of these species has involved determination for social ways of behaving that make individual or gathering endurance almost certain. The usually noticed Attachment conduct of little children remaining close to natural individuals would have had wellbeing benefits in the climate of early variation and enjoys comparable benefits today. Bowlby saw the climate of early variation as like current agrarian social orders. There is an endurance advantage in the ability to detect perhaps perilous circumstances like newness, being separated from everyone else, or fast methodology.

As per Bowlby, closeness trying to the Attachment figure despite danger is the "put forth objective" of the Attachment social framework.

Bowlby's unique record of a responsiveness period during which Attachments can type of between a half year and a few years has been changed by later scientists. These specialists have displayed there is without a doubt a delicate period during which Attachments will shape if conceivable, however the time span is more extensive and the impact less fixed and irreversible than first proposed.

With additional examination, creators talking about Attachment Theory have come to see the value in friendly improvement is impacted by later as well as prior Attachments. Early strides in Attachment occur most effectively in the event that the newborn child has one guardian, or a periodic consideration of few others. As indicated by Bowlby, nearly all along, numerous kids have more than one figure toward which they direct Attachment conduct. These figures are not treated the same; there is areas of strength for a for a youngster to coordinate Attachment conduct essentially toward one specific individual. Bowlby utilized the expression "monotropy" to depict this predisposition. Analysts and scholars have deserted this idea to the extent that it could be interpreted as meaning the relationship with the extraordinary figure contrasts subjectively from that of different figures. Rather, current reasoning proposes unmistakable progressive systems of Attachments.

Early encounters with guardians bit by bit lead to an arrangement of contemplations, recollections, convictions, assumptions, feelings, and ways of behaving about oneself as well as other people. This framework, called the "inside working model of social Attachments", keeps on creating with time and experience.

Inner models direct, decipher, and anticipate Attachment related conduct in oneself and the Attachment figure. As they foster in accordance with natural and formative changes, they consolidate the ability to reflect and impart about past and future Attachment Attachments. They empower the kid to deal with new kinds of social cooperations; knowing, for instance, a baby ought to be dealt with uniquely in contrast to a more established kid, or that communications with educators and guardians share qualities. Indeed, even cooperation with mentors share comparable qualities, as competitors who secure Attachment associations with their folks as well as their mentors will assume a part in the development of competitors in their imminent game. This inner working model keeps on creating through adulthood, assisting adapt to kinships, marriage, and life as a parent, all of which include various ways of behaving and sentiments.

The improvement of Attachment is a conditional interaction. Explicit Attachment ways of behaving start with unsurprising, obviously natural, ways of behaving in earliest stages. They change with age in manners decided part of the way by encounters and halfway by situational factors. As Attachment ways of behaving change with age, they do as such in manners molded by Attachments. A youngster's way of behaving when rejoined with a parental figure is resolved not just by how the guardian has treated the kid previously, yet on the historical backdrop of impacts the kid has had on the guardian.

CHAPTER THREE

The Independency Bluff

The mistaken conviction that all individuals ought to be sincerely independent isn't new. Quite recently in Western culture individuals accepted that youngsters would be more joyful assuming they were just let potentially run wild and educated to relieve themselves. Then Attachment Theory went along and turned these mentalities — essentially toward kids — around. During the 1940s specialists cautioned that "pampering" would bring about penniless and insecure youngsters who might turn out to be sincerely undesirable and maladjusted grown-ups. Guardians were told not to rich a lot of consideration on their newborn children, to permit them to sob for quite a long time and to prepare them to eat on an unforgiving timetable.

The normal conviction was that a legitimate distance ought to be kept up with among guardians and their kids, and that actual love ought to be given out sparingly. In Mental Consideration of Baby and Youngster, a famous nurturing book during the 1920s, John Broadus Watson cautioned against the risks of "an excess of mother love" and devoted the book "to the main mother who raises a cheerful kid." Such a kid would be an independent, dauntless, confident, versatile, critical thinking being who doesn't cry except if truly hurt, is caught up in work and play, and has no extraordinary Attachments to any place or individual.

The feelings, thought examples, and ways of behaving naturally set off in kids in Attachment circumstances show up in basically the same manner in grown-ups. The thing that matters is that grown-ups are equipped for a more elevated level of reflection, so our requirement for the other individual's ceaseless actual presence can on occasion be briefly supplanted by the information that they are accessible to us mentally and inwardly. In any case, basically the requirement for personal association and the consolation of our partner's accessibility keeps on assuming a significant part all through our lives.

Sadly, similarly as the significance of the parent-youngster bond was ignored previously, today the meaning of grown-up Attachment goes undervalued. Among grown-ups, the predominant idea is as yet that an excess of reliance in a relationship is something terrible.

The codependency development and other as of now famous self improvement approaches depict Attachments in a manner that is surprisingly like the perspectives held in the primary portion of the 20th 100 years about the youngster parent bond (recall the "blissful kid" who is liberated from pointless Attachments?). The present specialists offer exhortation that resembles this: Your satisfaction is something that ought to come from the inside and ought not be reliant upon your sweetheart or mate. Your prosperity isn't their obligation, and theirs isn't yours. Every individual necessities to take care of oneself. Moreover, you ought to learn not to permit your inward harmony to be upset by the individual you are nearest to. Assuming your partner acts in a manner that subverts your feeling of safety, you ought to have the option to fall limit any association with the circumstance inwardly, "maintain the emphasis on yourself," and remain on an even. In the event that you can't do that, there may be some kind of problem with you. You may be excessively enmeshed with the other individual, or mutually dependent and you should figure out how to define better limits."

The essential reason fundamental this perspective is that the ideal relationship is one between two independent individuals who join in a full grown, conscious way while keeping up with clear limits. In the event that you foster areas of strength for an on your partner, you are lacking somehow or another and are encouraged to deal with yourself to turn out to be more "separated" and create a "more noteworthy identity." The absolute worst situation is that you will wind up requiring your partner, which is compared with "compulsion" to the person in question, and enslavement, we as a whole know, is a perilous possibility.

While the lessons of the codependency development remain monstrously supportive in managing relatives who experience the ill effects of substance misuse (just like the underlying expectation), they can be deluding and, surprisingly, harming when applied unpredictably to all Attachments.

Various investigations show that once we become appended to somebody, both of us structure one physiological unit. Our partner controls our circulatory strain, our pulse, our breathing, and the degrees of chemicals in our blood. We are at this point not isolated elements. The accentuation on separation that is held by the greater part of the present well known brain research ways to deal with grown-up Attachments doesn't stand up to anything according to an organic viewpoint. Reliance is a reality; it's anything but a decision or an inclination.

The review exhibits that when two individuals structure a close Attachment, they direct each other's mental and profound prosperity. Their actual nearness and accessibility impact the pressure reaction. How might we be supposed to keep an elevated degree of separation among ourselves and our partners in the event that our essential science is impacted by them so much?

As per John Bowlby, our requirement for somebody to impart our lives to is important for our hereditary cosmetics and doesn't have anything to do with the amount we love ourselves or how satisfied we feel all alone. He found that once we pick somebody unique, strong and frequently wild powers become an integral factor. New examples of conduct kick in paying little mind to how free we are and in spite of our cognizant wills. When we pick an partner, there is no doubt about regardless of whether reliance exists. It generally does. A rich conjunction that does exclude awkward sensations of weakness and feeling of dread toward misfortune sounds great however isn't our science. What demonstrated through development to have areas of strength for a benefit is a human couple becoming one physiological unit, and that truly intends that in the event that she's responding, I'm responding, or on the other hand assuming he's bombshell, that likewise makes me disrupted. The person is essential for me, and I will effectively save the person in question; having such a personal stake in the prosperity of someone else converts into a vital endurance advantage for the two players.

In spite of varieties in the manner in which individuals with various Attachment styles figure out how to manage these strong powers — the protected and Anxious sorts embrace them and the avoidants will generally smother them — every one of the three Attachment styles are customized to interface with a unique somebody. Truth be told, part 6 depicts a progression of trials that show that avoidants have Attachment needs yet effectively stifle them.

Does this intend that to be content seeing someone should be gotten together with our partner at the hip or surrender different parts of our life like our professions or companions? Perplexingly, the inverse is valid! Incidentally, the capacity to step into the world all alone frequently comes from the information that there is somebody adjacent to us whom we can rely on — and this is the "reliance oddity." The rationale of this mystery is difficult to follow right away. How might we act more free by being completely reliant upon another person? In the event that we needed to depict the essential reason of grown-up Attachment in a solitary sentence, it would be:

If you have any desire to take the way to freedom and satisfaction, first track down the perfect individual to rely upon and travel down it with them. When you comprehend this, you've gotten a handle on the quintessence of Attachment Theory.

CHAPTER FOUR

Attachment Patterns/Styles

An individual's Attachment style is their particular approach to connecting with others in Relationships. Attachment style is molded and created in youth because of our associations with our earliest parental figures. Basically, our grown-up Attachment style is remembered to reflect the elements we had with our parental figures as babies and kids.

Attachment style incorporates the manner in which we answer genuinely to others as well as our ways of behaving and communications with them. The strength of a kid's Attachment conduct in a given situation doesn't demonstrate the 'strength' of the Attachment security. A few uncertain youngsters will regularly show extremely articulated Attachment ways of behaving, while many secure kids observe that there is no extraordinary need to participate in either serious or continuous shows of Attachment conduct. People with various Attachment styles have various convictions about heartfelt love period, accessibility, trust ability of affection partners and love preparation."

There are four primary grown-up Attachment styles: secure, Anxious, avoidant, and unfortunate avoidant. The last three are totally viewed as types of uncertain Attachment.

Secure Attachment
You're holding back nothing. It happens when guardians or different parental figures are:

- Available
- Touchy
- Responsive
- Tolerating

In associations with secure Attachment, guardians let their kids go all over town; however are there for them when they return for security and solace.

These guardians get their youngster, play with them, and console them when required. In this way, the youngster learns they can communicate pessimistic feelings and somebody will help them.

Kids who foster secure Attachment figure out how to trust and have solid confidence. Seems like rapture! As grown-ups, these kids are in contact with their sentiments, are skilled, and by and large have effective Attachments.

It alludes to the capacity to frame secure, adoring associations with others. A securely joined individual can trust others and be relied upon, affection and acknowledge love, and draw near to others no sweat. They're not terrified of closeness, nor do they feel overreacted when their partners need time or space away from them. They're ready to rely upon others without turning out to be absolutely reliant.

Around 56% of grown-ups have a protected Attachment type, as per essential Attachment research by friendly clinicians Cindy Hazan and Phillip Shaver during the 1980s.

Any remaining Attachment styles that are not secure are known as insecure Attachment styles.

Anxious Attachment
This sort of Attachment happens when guardians answer thekid's requirements irregularly. Care and security are some of the time there — and some of the time not.

In Anxious insecure Attachment, the kid can't depend on their folks to be there when required. Along these lines, the youngster neglects to foster any convictions that all is good from the Attachment figure.

Furthermore, since the kid can't depend on their parent to be there in the event that they feel undermined, they will not effectively get away from the parent to investigate.

The youngster turns out to be seriously requesting and even tenacious, trusting that their overstated trouble will drive the parent to respond.

In Anxious unreliable Attachment, the absence of consistency implies that the kid in the long run ends up being poor, furious, and skeptical.

It is a type of uncertain Attachment style set apart by a profound separation anxiety. Anxiously connected individuals will generally be exceptionally uncertain about their Attachments, frequently stressing that their partner will leave them and along these lines generally hungry for approval. Anxious Attachment is related with "destitution" or tenacious way of behaving, for example, getting extremely Anxious when your partner doesn't message back quickly enough and continually feeling like your partner couldn't care less about you.

Anxious Attachment is otherwise called Anxious distracted Attachment, and it by and large lines up with the Anxious irresolute Attachment style or Anxious safe Attachment style saw among kids. Some 19% of grown-ups have the Anxious Attachment type, as per Hazan and Shaver's exploration.

Avoidant Attachment
At times, a parent experiences difficulty tolerating and answering delicately to their kid's requirements. Rather than encouraging the kid, the parent:

- Limits their sentiments
- Rejects their requests
- Doesn't assist with troublesome undertakings

This prompts avoidant-insecure Attachment.

Likewise, the kid might be supposed to assist the parent with their own necessities. The youngster discovers that trying not to carry the parent into the picture is ideal. All things considered, the parent doesn't answer in a supportive way.

In avoidant-unreliable Attachment, the kid discovers that their smartest choice is to close down their sentiments and become confident.

Ainsworth showed that youngsters with an avoidant-uncertain Attachment won't go to the parent when they're troubled and attempt to limit showing pessimistic feelings.

It is a type of unreliable Attachment style set apart by a feeling of dread toward closeness. Individuals with avoidant Attachment style will generally experience difficulty drawing near to other people or confiding in others in Attachments, and Attachments can cause them to feel choked. They commonly avoid their partners or are to a great extent relationally stunted in their Attachments, liking to be free and depend on themselves.

Avoidant Attachment is otherwise called contemptuous avoidant Attachment, and it by and large lines up with the Anxious avoidant Attachment style saw among kids. Some 25% of grown-ups have the avoidant Attachment type, as per Hazan and Shaver.

Fearful-Avoidant Attachment (Disorganized)
Around 15% of children in group with low psychosocial risk — and upwards of 82% of those in high-risk circumstances — foster disorganized insecure attachment.

For this situation, guardians show abnormal way of behaving: They reject, criticize, and scare their youngster.

Guardians who show these ways of behaving frequently have a previous that incorporates unsettled injury. Unfortunately, when the kid moves toward the parent, they feel dread and expanded uneasiness rather than care and security.

The initial three Attachment styles are at times alluded to as "coordinated." That is on the grounds that the kid figures out how they need to appropriately act and sorts out their technique.

This fourth Attachment style, notwithstanding, is thought of "muddled" on the grounds that the youngster's procedure is disrupted — as is their subsequent way of behaving.

In the end, the kid begins to foster ways of behaving that assist them with having a real sense of reassurance. For instance, the youngster may:

- Become forceful toward the parent
- Decline care from the parent
- Essentially become very confident

It is a mix of both the anxious and avoidant Attachment styles. Individuals with unfortunate avoidant Attachment both frantically ache for love and need to keep away from it no matter what. They're hesitant to foster a nearby heartfelt Attachment, but simultaneously, they have a desperate need to feel cherished by others.

Unfortunate avoidant Attachment is otherwise called muddled Attachment, and it's moderately intriguing and not well-informed. In any case, we in all actuality do realize it's related with huge mental and social dangers, including elevated sexual way of behaving, an expanded gamble for savagery in their Attachments, and trouble controlling feelings overall.

CHAPTER FIVE

Attachment Pattern/Styles in Adults

Attachment Theory was reached out to grown-up close Attachments in the last part of the 1980s by Cindy Hazan and Phillip Shaver. Four styles of Attachment have been distinguished in grown-ups: secure, Anxious distracted, cavalier avoidant and unfortunate avoidant. These generally relate to baby orders: secure, uncertain undecided, insecure avoidant and scattered/perplexed.

Securely Attached
Securely attached adults have been "linked to a serious requirement for accomplishment and a low anxiety toward disappointment. They will emphatically move toward an errand determined to dominate it and have a craving for investigation in accomplishment settings. Research shows that securely connected grown-ups have a "low degree of individual misery and elevated degrees of worry for other people". Because of their high paces of self-viability, securely joined grown-ups normally feel free to an individual having an adverse

consequence from risky circumstances they are confronting. This quiet reaction is illustrative of the securely joined grown-up's sincerely controlled reaction to dangers that many examinations have upheld despite assorted circumstances. Grown-up secure Attachment comes from a person's initial association with their caregiver(s), qualities and their heartfelt encounters.

Anxious-Preoccupied

Anxious preoccupied grown-ups look for elevated degrees of closeness, endorsement and responsiveness from partners, turning out to be excessively reliant. They will generally be less trusting, have more negative perspectives about themselves and their partners, and may display elevated degrees of profound expressiveness, stress and imprudence in their Attachments. The nervousness that grown-ups feel forestalls the foundation of good safeguard rejection. Along these lines, it is conceivable that people that have been tensely appended to their Attachment figure or figures have not had the option to foster adequate safeguards against fearing abandonment. In light of their absence of readiness these people will then go overboard to the expectation of division or the genuine detachment from their Attachment figure. The uneasiness comes from a person's extraordinary as well as unsteady relationship that leaves the Anxious or distracted individual somewhat vulnerable. Grown-ups with this Attachment style frequently project their tensions onto in any case harmless social communications, paying little heed to on the off chance that the cooperation is up close and personal or through a text-based medium like texting or email. Their contemplations and activities can prompt a difficult pattern of unavoidable outcomes, conceivably prompting self destructive behavior.

Dismissive-Avoidant

Contemptuous avoidant grown-ups want an elevated degree of freedom, frequently seeming to stay away from Attachment by and large. They view themselves as independent, safe to Attachment sentiments and not requiring cozy Attachments. They will generally smother their sentiments, managing struggle by limiting any association with partners of whom they frequently have an unfortunate assessment. Grown-ups come up short on interest of framing cozy Attachments and keeping up with profound closeness with individuals around them. They have a lot of doubt in others and yet have a positive model of self, they would like to put resources into their own self image abilities. Due to their doubt they can't be persuaded that others can convey daily reassurance. They attempt to make elevated degrees of confidence by putting excessively in their capacities or achievements. These grown-ups keep up with their good perspectives on self, in view of their own accomplishments and skill as opposed to looking for and feeling acknowledgment from others. These grown-ups will unequivocally dismiss or limit the significance of profound Attachment and inactively keep away from Attachments when they feel like they are turning out to be excessively close. They take a stab at confidence and freedom. With regards to the assessments of others about themselves, they are exceptionally impassive and are generally reluctant to positive input from their companions. Cavalier aversion can likewise be made sense of as the consequence of guarded deactivation of the Attachment framework to stay away from expected dismissal, or certified negligence for relational closeness.

Fearful-Avoidant

Fearful avoidant grown-ups have blended sentiments about cozy Attachments, both wanting and feeling awkward with profound closeness. The hazardous part about the differentiation between needing to shape social Attachments while at the same time dreading the relationship is that it makes psychological dysfunction. This psychological maladjustment then, at that point, converts into doubting the Attachments they truly do frame and furthermore seeing themselves as shameful. Moreover, unfortunate avoidant grown-ups likewise have a less lovely point of view contrasted with Anxious distracted and contemptuous avoidant gatherings. Like contemptuous avoidant grown-ups, unfortunate avoidant grown-ups will generally look for less closeness, stifling their sentiments.

CHAPTER SIX

How to Identify your Attachment Style/Pattern

Here is a basic Attachment style test to distinguish your own Attachment style. As a rule, however, many individuals can peruse the portrayals of the four Attachment styles and naturally perceive themselves in one of them. Here is a speedy stomach check for you: Underneath are the portrayals of the primary Attachment types utilized in Hazan and Shaver's fundamental examination on Attachment Theory. Peruse the assertions and pick the one that most impacts you:

- I find it generally simple to draw near to other people and am happy with relying upon them and having them rely upon me. I don't frequently stress over being deserted or about somebody getting excessively near me.
- I observe that others are hesitant to get as close as I would like. I frequently stress that my partner doesn't actually cherish me or won't have any desire to remain

with me. I need to combine totally with someone else, and this want at times frightens individuals off.
- I'm to some degree awkward being near others; I find it challenging to trust them totally, hard to permit myself to rely upon them. I'm anxious when anybody gets excessively close, and frequently, love partners maintain that I should be more private than I feel open to being.

Significantly, it's likewise conceivable to have an alternate Attachment style in various circumstances.

While we might have an essential Attachment style, contingent upon our Attachments, we might have a solid sense of reassurance with one individual than we do with another. For some individuals, their Attachment style isn't similar in each relationship they experience. Things that add to this are their partner's (heartfelt or non-romantic) character and convictions that all is good.

Secure Attachment Style
Secure Attachment is the consequence of having a solid sense of safety with your guardians from youth and having the option to request consolation

or approval without discipline. Eventually, you had a real sense of reassurance, comprehended, helped, and esteemed during your initial collaborations. Your parental figures were most likely sincerely accessible and mindful of their own feelings and ways of behaving.

Indications of a Secure Attachment style include:

- Capacity to manage your feelings
- Effectively confiding in others
- Viable relational abilities
- Capacity to look for basic encouragement
- Open to being distant from everyone else
- Agreeable in cozy Attachments
- Capacity to self-reflect in associations
- Being not difficult to interface with
- Capacity to oversee struggle well
- High confidence
- Capacity to be genuinely accessible

Avoidant Attachment Style

Avoidant, dismissive-avoidant, or Anxious avoidant are words for a similar unreliable Attachment style. It's characterized by disappointments to construct long haul associations with others because of a failure to take part in physical and close to home closeness. In adolescence, you might have had severe or sincerely far off and missing parental figures. Your guardians might have:

- Passed on you to battle for yourself
- Anticipated that you should be autonomous
- Censured you for relying upon them
- Dismissed you while communicating your requirements or feelings
- Been delayed to answer your essential necessities
- Some avoidant-delivering guardians are out and out careless however others are just occupied, marginally unbiased, and more worried about things like grades, tasks, or habits than sentiments, expectations, dreams, or fears.
- Thus, these kids might figure out how to take on major areas of strength for an of freedom so they don't need to depend on any other individual for care or backing.

Indications of Avoidant Attachment Style; you could have a Anxious avoidant Attachment style if you:

- Constantly stay away from profound or actual closeness

- Feel areas of strength for an of freedom
- Are awkward communicating your sentiments
- Are pompous of others
- Struggle with confiding in individuals
- Feel undermined by any individual who attempts to draw near to you
- Invest more energy alone than connecting with others
- Accept you don't require others in your life
- Responsibility issues

Anxious Attachment Style
Anxious Attachment style is described by:

- Apprehension about dismissal
- Separation anxiety
- Contingent upon an partner for approval and profound guideline
- Mutually dependent inclinations

This Attachment style originates from conflicting nurturing that isn't sensitive to a youngster's requirements. These youngsters experience issues grasping their guardians and have no security for what's in store from them pushing ahead. They're in many cases confounded inside their parental Attachments and feel unsteady.

Youngsters with this Attachment style experience exceptionally high misery when their parental figures leave. In some cases, the guardians will be strong and receptive to the youngster's requirements while at different times, they won't be sensitive to their kids.

In the event that you have a Anxious Attachment style, your folks might have moreover:

- Shifted back and forth between being excessively indulging and separated or detached
- Been effortlessly wrecked
- Been some of the time mindful and afterward drive you away
- Made you answerable for how they felt
- In this way, these youngsters frequently grow up thinking they should deal with others' sentiments and frequently become mutually dependent.

Signs you could have a Anxious Attachment style include:

- Tenacious inclinations
- Exceptionally delicate to analysis (genuine or saw)
- Requiring endorsement from others

- Envious propensities
- Trouble being separated from everyone else
- Low confidence
- Feeling dishonorable of adoration
- Extreme feeling of dread toward dismissal
- Critical separation anxiety
- Trouble confiding in others

Disorganized Attachment Style

Anxious confused Attachment is characterized as having incredibly conflicting way of behaving and trouble confiding in others. The most well-known reasons for a scattered Attachment style are youth injury, disregard, or misuse. Feeling of dread toward their folks (their feeling of safety) is likewise present.

Kids with this Attachment style might appear to be confounded. Guardians are conflicting and are frequently viewed as wellsprings of solace and dread by their kids, which prompts their disarranged ways of behaving.

Indications of a complicated Attachment style include:

- Apprehension about dismissal

- Powerlessness to manage feelings
- Incongruous ways of behaving
- Elevated degrees of nervousness
- Trouble confiding in others
- Indications of both avoidant and Anxious Attachment styles

This type is additionally connected with emotional well-being conditions in adulthood, including:

- Mind-set issues
- Behavioral conditions
- Self-hurt
- Substance use.

CHAPTER SEVEN

How your Attachment Pattern/Style affects your Relationship

Socially, insecure people will generally be cooperated with uncertain people, and secure people with secure people. Insecure Attachments will generally be persevering yet less sincerely fulfilling contrasted with the relationship(s) of two securely joined people.

Attachment styles are enacted from the primary date onwards and influence relationship elements and how a relationship closes. Secure Attachment has been displayed to consider better compromise in a relationship and for one's capacity to leave an unsuitable relationship contrasted with other Attachment types. Secure people's true high confidence and positive perspective on others takes into account this as they are certain that they will track down another relationship. Secure Attachment has likewise displayed to consider the effective handling of social misfortunes (for example demise, dismissal, treachery, surrender and so forth) Attachment has additionally been displayed to affect providing care conduct in Attachments.

How Secure Attachment Style appears in Relationships

Within romantic relationships, a securely joined grown-up will show up in the accompanying ways: magnificent compromise, intellectually adaptable, powerful communicators, evasion of control, OK with closeness without frightfulness of being enmeshed, rapidly lenient, seeing sex and profound closeness as one, accepting they can decidedly influence their relationship, and really focusing on their partner in the manner they need to be really focused on. In summation, they are extraordinary partners who treat their mates quite well, as they won't hesitate to give decidedly and request their should be met. Securely appended grown-ups accept that there are "numerous potential partners that would be receptive to their requirements", and in the event that they a not go over a person addressing their necessities, they will normally lose interest rapidly. In a review contrasting secure-endlessly secure different Attachment style Attachments, there was no vacillation in certain social working. In any case, in any blend of two partners with Attachment styles beyond secure, the Attachments showed elevated degrees of negative relationship working. This exploration demonstrates that it just takes one securely joined partner inside a close Attachment to keep up with solid, profound relationship working.

Securely joined individuals grow up having a solid sense of reassurance sincerely and truly and can take part on the planet with others in a sound manner.

Subsequently, individuals with secure Attachment styles will generally explore Attachments well. They're by and large certain, trusting, and wanting to their partners.

They trust their partners' expectations and envy is in many cases not an issue for them. Securely connected individuals feel that they genuinely deserve love and don't require outer consolation.

How Avoidant Attachment Style appears in Relationships
Anxious avoidant appended grown-ups may will more often than not explore Attachments at a careful distance. The requirement for profound

closeness is basically ailing in this kind of individual, so heartfelt Attachments can't arrive at any degree of profundity.

While they permit significant others to draw in with them, they try not to get sincerely close. Partner might feel as though they can never get inside and will unavoidably be stone-walled or excused when the relationship feels excessively intense for the Anxious avoidant partner.

How Anxious Attachment Style appears in Relationships
Individuals with Anxious Attachment styles generally feel shameful of affection and need steady consolation from their partners. They frequently fault themselves for challenges in the relationship and can show continuous and serious desire or doubt because of unfortunate confidence.

Eventually, there's a well established feeling of dread toward being deserted, dismissed, or alone. What's more, those fears ordinarily communicate their thoughts in these ways.

How Disorganized Attachment Style manifests in Relationships

In Attachments, individuals with muddled Attachment styles will generally have flighty and befuddling conduct. They shift back and forth between being reserved and autonomous and being tenacious and profound. While they frantically look for adoration, they additionally drive partners away due to the apprehension about affection. They accept that they'll constantly be dismissed, however they don't stay away from profound closeness. They dread it, and they additionally reliably search it out, just to dismiss it once more. They see their partners as erratic, and they personally act in unusual ways inside their Attachments as they keep on wrestling between the requirement for security and dread.

CHAPTER EIGHT

Assessing and Measuring Attachment

Two primary parts of grown-up Attachment have been contemplated. The association and strength of the psychological working models that underlie the Attachment styles is investigated by friendly analysts inspired by heartfelt Attachment. Formative clinicians keen on the singular's perspective regarding Attachment by and large investigate what Attachment capabilities in relationship elements and means for relationship results. The association of mental working models is more steady while the singular's perspective concerning Attachment changes more. A few creators have recommended that grown-ups don't hold a solitary arrangement of working models. All things being equal, on one level they have a bunch of rules and suppositions about Attachment Attachments overall. On one more level they hold data about unambiguous Attachments or relationship occasions. Data at various levels need not be predictable. People can in this manner hold different inward working models for various Attachments.

There are various proportions of grown-up Attachment, the most well-known being self-report surveys and coded interviews in light of the Grown-up Attachment Interview. The different measures were grown basically as exploration devices, for various purposes and tending to various areas, for instance heartfelt Attachments, dispassionate Attachments, parental Attachments or friend Attachments. Some characterize a grown-up's perspective as for Attachment and Attachment designs by reference to adolescence encounters, while others evaluate relationship ways of behaving and security in regards to guardians and friends.

Associations of Adult Attachment with other Traits
Grown-up Attachment styles are connected with individual contrasts in the ways in which grown-ups insight and deal with their feelings. Late meta-examinations connect unreliable Attachment styles to bring down capacity to appreciate individuals on a profound level and lower quality care.

CHAPTER NINE

Can your Attachment Style change?

Indeed, it is feasible for an individual to change their connection style. Be that as it may, this takes a ton of work, persistence, and goal assuming an individual is moving from an uncertain to a safe connection methodology.

The following are a couple of ways of beginning:

Distinguish your relationship patterns.
Begin by pondering your relationship with your folks as a youngster. Ask yourself inquiries like:

- How were they toward you as a kid?
- How could you answer them?
- To whom did you go for solace when you had an issue?
- Is it true or not that they were careless or solid?

This will assist you with getting greater clearness on what might have molded your connection style.

Survey your current and past connection style and recognize assuming that there are any examples in picking significant others. Know about your young life history; the commonality is encouraging, whether it was fortunate or unfortunate. Meaning, your past unfortunate relationship designs from youth can reproduce in adulthood.

Work on your Confidence.
Low confidence is a typical trademark across all unreliable connection styles.

Figure out how to embrace, worth, love, and care for yourself first," she suggests. "In the event that you can't comprehend what self esteem is on the grounds that you were ignored, manhandled, and excused as a kid, you can begin with self-resistance and self-lack of bias. This can seem to be, 'I'm an individual, and everybody should be esteemed' as opposed to constraining yourself with meaningless statements of, 'I'm wonderful and important.'"

Reach out to your genuine requirements.
By the day's end, all shaky connection styles are individuals who will more often than not structure uncertain connections due to profoundly held fears that their connections won't work out. So it means a lot to sort out some way to cause yourself to have a good sense of safety in your connections. Some portion of that includes monitoring what your necessities and wants are seeing someone.

Figure out how to be confident and defined limits. Honor what you feel, and express your necessities in words without control and profound implications. Safely joined individuals are frequently immediate and suitably fierce to make a solid and significant relationship.

Feel free to seek therapy.
Therapy is useful, both individual and couples. A quality specialist will assist you with plunging into your connection style, past injuries, ways of recognizing, lay out proper limits, and advance a solid relationship.

CONCLUSION

Nurturing is tied in with chiseling a future for your kid. Plan to show up for them — genuinely and actually — and you can energize the solid attachment that prompts the best ways of behaving in adulthood.

Just sit back and relax in the event that you don't necessarily in all cases hit the nail on the head. Also, assuming you feel that you might want to pursue changing your own Attachment style, recollect that nothing is cut in stone.

Printed in Great Britain
by Amazon